SALINE DISTRICT LIBRARY

W9-ASH-599

JE394.26   Mar
Marx, David F.
Kwanzaa

WITHDRAWN

Read-About® Holidays

Kwanzaa

By David F. Marx

Consultant
Katharine A. Kane, Reading Specialist
Former Language Arts Coordinator
San Diego County Office of Education

SALINE DISTRICT LIBRARY
555 N. Maple Road
Saline, MI 48176

Children's Press®
A Division of Grolier Publishing
New York   London   Hong Kong   Sydney
Danbury, Connecticut

Visit Children's Press® on the Internet at:
http://publishing.grolier.com

Designer: Herman Adler Design Group
Photo Researcher: Caroline Anderson

Library of Congress Cataloging-in-Publication Data

Marx, David F.
    Kwanzaa / by David F. Marx.
        p. cm. — (Rookie read-about holidays)
    Includes index.
    Summary: Introduces the history, customs, meaning, and
celebration of Kwanzaa.
    ISBN 0-516-22207-4 (lib. bdg.)   0-516-27155-5 (pbk.)
    1. Kwanzaa—Juvenile literature. [1. Kwanzaa. 2. Afro-Americans—
Social life and customs. 3. Holidays.] I. Title.
GT4403.M35   2000
394.261—dc21
                                            00-022635

©2000 Children's Press®
A Division of Grolier Publishing Co., Inc.
All rights reserved. Published simultaneously in Canada.
Printed in the United States of America.
1 2 3 4 5 6 7 8 9 10 R 09 08 07 06 05 04 03 02 01 00

Do you celebrate Kwanzaa?

African-Americans have celebrated this winter holiday for more than thirty years.

Kwanzaa was created in 1966 by an African-American man named Maulana Karenga.

Maulana Karenga

December 2000

Sunday	Monday	Tuesday	Wednesday	Thursday	Friday	Saturday
					1	2
3	4	5	6	7	8	9
10	11	12	13	14	15	16
17	18	19	20	21	22	23
24/31	25	26	27	28	29	30

Kwanzaa begins on
December 26. It lasts
for seven days.

People in the United States,
Canada, and many other
countries celebrate it.

"Kwanzaa" is a Swahili (swah-HEEL-ee) word. Swahili is a language spoken in parts of Africa.

Kwanzaa is a holiday that honors African culture.

Playing African music at a Kwanzaa celebration

During Kwanzaa, people think about seven important principles. Principles are ideas that help us lead good and honest lives.

The seven principles of Kwanzaa are:

- Unity
- Self-determination
- Collective work and responsibility
- Cooperative economics
- Purpose
- Creativity
- Faith

Families gather on each night of Kwanzaa to honor a different principle.

They read stories, sing songs, and light candles.

13

14

This is a special candle-
holder for Kwanzaa.
It is called a kinara
(KEE-nah-rah).

It holds seven candles, one
for each principle. One
candle is black, three are
red, and three are green.

The kinara is placed
on a straw mat called
a mkeka (m-KAY-cah).

Ears of corn called
muhindi (moo-HEEN-dee)
are also placed on the
mkeka. There is one ear
of corn for each child in
a family.

mkeka

18

Other fruits and vegetables are placed on the mat. They are reminders of foods grown in Africa.

Families share a large
unity cup called a
kikombe (KEE-kohm-bay).

Unity means living
and working happily
with others.

Kwanzaa brings a lot
of people together!

kikombe

During Kwanzaa, some parents give children gifts called zawadi (sah-WAH-dee).

Many of these gifts are handmade.

On the last night of Kwanzaa, there is a big celebration called karamu (kar-ah-MOO).

Some people dress in African clothes. There is a lot of joyful singing and dancing.

"Harambee!"

What does that mean?

It is a Swahili word
meaning, "Let's all
pull together!"

During Kwanzaa, you don't hear "Harambee" just one time. It is called out seven times in a row. It is a happy word. It brings everyone together.

"Harambee!"
"Harambee!"
"Harambee!"
"Harambee!"
"Harambee!"
"Harambee!"
"Harambee!"

Words You Know

karamu

kikombe

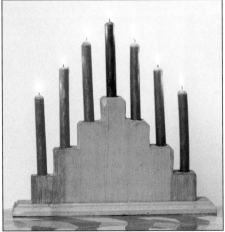

kinara

30

mkeka

muhindi

zawadi

31

Index

About the Author

David F. Marx is an author and editor of children's books.
He resides in the Chicago area.

Photo Credits

Photographs ©: AP/Wide World Photos: 25, 30 top (Lynsey Addario),
5 (Damian Dovarganes), 9 (Susan Goldman); International Stock Photo/
Patrick Ramsey: 26; PhotoEdit/Pat Olear: 3, 21, 30 bottom left; Stock
Boston/Lawrence Migdale 10, 13, 14, 17, 18, 22, 30 bottom right, 31;
Superstock, Inc.: cover, 29.